Justified Humanitarian Intervention: Operation ALLIED FORCE

1

Executive Summary

Title: Justified Humanitarian Intervention: Operation Allied Force

Author: Major Carol Yeager, United States Air Force Reserve

Thesis: Traditional U.S. doctrine on the use of force is inadequate to address the unique circumstances surrounding humanitarian interventions. Without specific doctrine to guide decision makers, it is too easy to make errors and hasty judgments that can cost the lives and treasure of both our citizens and people around the world. The United States must develop doctrine to guide decisions on the proper use of military force for humanitarian intervention prior to facing a crisis. The Responsibility to Protect doctrine provides U.S. decision makers with a tool to determine our nation's best course of action in upholding human rights and promoting our national interests.

Discussion: The decision to intervene in a humanitarian crisis is never easy. It requires forethought and a clear process that takes both international law and moral responsibility into consideration. NATO's Operation ALLIED FORCE serves as an informative case study to evaluate issues of sovereignty and the ethical responsibility of the international community to safeguard the lives of people around the world. The Responsibility to Protect doctrine provides a framework for the decision making process. According to the Responsibility to Protect doctrine, developed nations are justified in intervening in foreign nations when a government violates the human rights of its citizens. The question is not whether intervention is justifiable but rather when, how, and under what conditions a nation may violate the territory of another nation. In addition, historical precedents and arguments in favor and opposed to intervention must be included in the decision making process for the United States in future crises.

Conclusion: The United States has and will continue to face situations similar to that of Kosovo in 1999. Any justification to intervene must be based on sound decision making with an emphasis on concern for protecting human rights and promoting justice. Although military force may be a necessary response to humanitarian crises, other approaches must be exhausted prior to resorting to the use of force. As a world leader, the United States must establish a clear, ethical process to address humanitarian crises in order to provide guidance for our leaders and to serve as a model for the international community.

Table of Contents

DISCLAIMER

THE OPINIONS AND CONCLUSIONS EXPRESSED HEREIN ARE THOSE OF THE INDIVIDUAL STUDENT AUTHOR AND DO NOT NECESSARILY REPRESENT THE VIEWS OF EITHER THE MARINE CORPS COMMAND AND STAFF COLLEGE OR ANY OTHER GOVERNMENTAL AGENCY. REFERENCES TO THIS STUDY SHOULD INCLUDE THE FOREGOING STATEMENT.

QUOTATION FROM, ABSTRACTION FROM, OR REPRODUCTION OF ALL OR ANY PART OF THIS DOCUMENT IS PERMITTED PROVIDED PROPER ACKNOWLEDGEMENT IS MADE.

Acknowledgements

I am grateful to Dr Paul Gelpi for his insight and guidance throughout this research project. I also want to thank Dr Rebecca Johnson for her early insights into the Responsibility to Protect doctrine and direction in my research. I also wish to express gratitude to Dr Paolo Tripodi for his willingness to review and discuss the ethical issues raised in this paper and his suggestions of resources that contributed to this final written paper.

Finally I must recognize the support of my husband Gregory and children Samuel and Abigail. Your encouragement and patience during the many hours of my reading and writing limited our time together as a family and through it all you continued to believe in me and supported my efforts. Thank you!

Introduction

From Rwanda in 1994 to Somalia, Bosnia, Kosovo, Libya and Syria today, scholars, humanitarians, and politicians have debated the question of the use of military force to address a humanitarian crisis. Instances of human rights violations committed by governments against their own people are not a new phenomenon nor will such atrocities go away in the future. The inconsistent international response to these crises, challenges to international law, and changing norms complicate the decision making process on humanitarian intervention. International approaches vary from no intervention to United Nations Security Council (UNSC) resolutions denouncing such actions to diplomatic efforts and even the use of military force. The varied responses and changes in international norms can leave the international community with inadequate guidance to decide upon the best course of action for intervention. The Responsibility to Protect (R2P) doctrine is one attempt to address this issue. The UN SC first applied the R2P doctrine to its resolution on Darfur in 2006, and more recently in 2011 in Resolution 1973 to endorse a no-fly zone over Libya. However, there is still disagreement over R2P and the traditional international understanding of State sovereignty.

Currently, the United States' response to humanitarian crises leans towards support of R2P doctrine. Nevertheless, U.S. responses vary with each crisis. It has chosen both to intervene and not. It has relied on both diplomatic efforts including negotiations and sanctions but it also used military force. The inconsistency in the U.S. approach highlights the lack of a clear doctrine to inform the decision on the use of force in humanitarian intervention. It also reflects the tension within the U.S. between a history of non-intervention and perception of itself as the world's guardian and promoter of human rights. Traditional U.S. doctrine on the use of force is inadequate to address the unique circumstances surrounding humanitarian interventions. Without specific doctrine to guide decision makers, it is too easy to make errors and hasty judgments that can cost the lives and treasure of both our citizens and people around the world. The United States must develop doctrine to guide decisions on the proper use of military force for humanitarian intervention prior to facing a crisis. R2P doctrine provides U.S. decision makers with a tool to determine our nation's best course of action in upholding human rights and promoting our national interests.

The Responsibility to Protect doctrine and western Just War theory are good starting places but are not sufficient on their own; historical precedence and national security concerns must also be considered. This paper will examine Operation ALLIED FORCE as a case study of U.S. and NATO decision-making concerning humanitarian intervention and its consequences. It will also address traditional U.S. approaches to the use of force and the reason such doctrines fail to address situations involving human rights violations within a sovereign state. Finally, guidelines for developing U.S. doctrine will be presented.

Historical Overview of Conflict in Kosovo

In order to understand the war in Kosovo, an historical overview of the territory is helpful. For centuries Serbians and ethnic Albanians have disagreed over territorial claims to Kosovo. Both claims are based on historical myths and reflect the enduring rivalry between ethnic Albanians living in Kosovo and Serbians.

The importance of Kosovo to Serbian national identity cannot be overstated. Serbians view Kosovo as the birthplace of their culture and the spiritual center of the medieval Serbian Empire. [1] The Serbians first arrived in the territory in the 4th century and by the late 12th century Kosovo was filled with Serbian Orthodox churches and monasteries. In contrast to the Serb claims, ethnic Albanians living in Kosovo cite their Illyrian ancestry and population majority in their claim to the land.

In 1385 the area fell under Ottoman rule and four years later the Serbians unsuccessfully fought their rulers at the battle of Kosovo Polje (also known as Vidovdan). As historian Alexsander Pavkovic noted "Kosovo came to signify the struggle for the freedom of the Serbs…[it] has become the main symbol and focus of the national liberation of the Serbian lands from foreign rule…."[2]

Following the defeat of the Serbs in 1389, Islam came to the area along with the rise of the Ottoman Empire and their rule over the Balkans. Many ethnic Albanians living in Kosovo recognized the benefits of conversion and joined the faith. By virtue of their conversion, the ethnic Albanians gained influence and power in Kosovo. In contrast, Serbians did not convert to Islam and migrated north during this time. Their emigration altered the ethnic makeup of Kosovo leaving it largely inhabited by ethnic Albanians thereby furthering their claims to the land.

Following the disintegration of the Ottoman Empire at the end of World War I, much disagreement and conflict over the status of the Balkan states existed resulting in a series of Balkan Wars that took place from 1874-1913. During this time, Serbian nationalism grew and although an independent Albanian state existed, "much of the Albanian ethnic space, Kosovo included, was occupied by Serbian and Greek armies."[3] The occupation led to discontent among the majority of ethnic Albanians living in Kosovo. Some Albanian historians argue that during this time the Serbian government actively tried to change the majority population in Kosovo through killings, forced expulsion, and colonization. "As a consequence of ethnic cleansing and colonization of the Albanian land, a significant change of the ethnic structure of the population resulted. While the Albanians comprised 90% of the population in these regions in 1912, it was down to 70 % in 1941."[4]

During World War II, Italy created the territory of Greater Albania that included Kosovo. Many Kosovars assumed their homeland would remain a part of Albania following the war. Instead the nation of Yugoslavia was reestablished and Kosovo once again fell under Serb control. Following the war Josip Broz "Tito," a Croatian by birth, came to power in Yugoslavia. Under his leadership he allowed the Kosovars a measure of limited independence and until 1966 treated the territory as an autonomous region within Yugoslavia. In 1974, "Kosovo was bestowed a constitution separate from that of the Serbia, the status of the Socialist Autonomous Province with rights equal to those of the nations of Yugoslavia." [5]

The Break Up of Yugoslavia

Following Tito's death in 1980, Yugoslavia continued to operate under a collective government; however, ethnic tensions and an increase in nationalist sentiment in the various regions of Yugoslavia threatened its unity. The U.S. Department of State, in the spring of 1990 stated that democratic elections resulted in "nationalist and independence- minded governments" coming to power in Slovenia, Croatia and Serbia." [6] As a result of these elections, Croatia and Slovenia declared their independence from Yugoslavia and Serb dominance. The region suffered four years of war between these new "states" and Serbia. Bosnia followed its neighbors and declared its independence from Yugoslavia in 1992. This war lasted until late 1995. In response to these independence movements, the European community recognized Croatia and Slovenia's independence in January 1992 and in April of the same year recognized Bosnia as an independent state despite resistance by the Serbs living in Bosnia. Violence and human rights violations increased during this time. In an effort to contain the violence and prevent further human rights abuses, the UN stationed international observation forces in the territory. However, the UN restricted these observers use of force to self defense only and they stood by helplessly as Serbian forces conducted a brutal campaign of human rights violations throughout Bosnia. Finally, in 1994, the UN authorized NATO air strikes against Bosnian Serb forces in order to protect UN established safe havens. These air strikes eventually convinced Yugoslav President Slobodan Milosevic to cease hostilities and sign the Dayton Peace Agreement on November 30, 1995.

Kosovo's Bid for Independence

Milosevic rose to political power largely on calls for a renewed Serbian nationalism. As part of this Serb nationalism, Milosevic altered the Serbian constitution in 1989 to limit Kosovo's autonomy. These constitutional changes, along with the successful independence movements in Croatia, Slovenia, and Bosnia-Herzegovina motivated the ethnic Albanians to hold unofficial elections and establish a shadow government in Kosovo. The Kosovars expected international recognition of their independence just as they witnessed in the earlier cases of Slovenia, Croatia, and Bosnia. Unfortunately for the ethnic Albanians the international community didn't respond.

While the international community focused on the war in Bosnia-Herzegovina, the conflict and violence grew in Kosovo. For several years Kosovars protested Milosevic's changes using non-violent means. However, as time went by and no international support for an independent Kosovo developed, many ethnic Albanians lost faith in non-violent resistance efforts. The Kosovo Liberation Army (KLA) was born out of this frustration. The KLA carried out small attacks against the Yugoslav Army and police forces in an effort to draw attention to the plight of ethnic Albanians within Kosovo and push the Serbs out of the land. In response to these KLA attacks, Serb forces increased their oppression of and brutal attacks on Kosovars. Milosevic responded brutally to the ethnic Albanian independence efforts. He explained his violent response in his October 1998 comment to the NATO Commander General Wesley Clark stating, "You know, General Clark, we know how to handle the problems with these Albanian killers... We have done this before [in] Drenica 1946....We kill them, all of them."[7]

UN and NATO Response to the Conflict in Kosovo

Based upon their experience in Bosnia the United Nations and NATO feared an increase in violence in Kosovo. By September 1998 the Kosovo crisis prompted the UN Secretary General to send a letter to Milosevic demanding that he take immediate steps to end the violence and destruction in Kosovo. The UN Security Council (UNSC) followed up this letter on September 23 with resolution 1199 "reaffirming its commitment to support a peaceful resolution to the Kosovo problem."[8] This resolution viewed the Kosovo situation "as a threat to peace and stability in the region" and empowered the "Council to act under Chapter VII of the Charter." [9] On January 15, 1999 the Kosovo Verification Force (unarmed observers from the Organization for the Security and Cooperation in Europe) reported a massacre at Racak, where Serbian irregular forces apparently killed 45 ethnic Albanian citizens. The massacre triggered the "abandonment by the United States of its policy of attempting to preserve stability in the former Yugoslavia"[10] and solidified the western view that Serbia, especially Milosevic, was at fault for the atrocities and conflict in Kosovo and that something must be done to stop the violence.

In response to the massacre report, U.S. Secretary of State Madeline Albright demanded

Serbia and Kosovar officials meet and hold diplomatic talks to end the violence. In February

1999 the two sides and the U.S. met near Paris at Rambouillet. The U.S. attempted to force a

solution to the Kosovo crisis and establish temporary provision for an independent Kosovo in the

future. The Rambouillet Accords also demanded the ethnic Albanians cease attacks upon

Serbian forces in the territory. The Albanians reluctantly agreed and signed the accord.

However, the Serbians refused to agree to the terms, in part because they opposed the presence

of NATO troops in Kosovo but also because the agreement directly conflicted with their view

towards Kosovo as a part of Serbia. This refusal was the last straw for NATO and signaled the

breakdown of peace talks. Convinced that Milosevic was the source of the problem and that a

failure to intervene would lead to further civilian deaths and massacres, the North Atlantic

Council (NAC), the political decision making arm of NATO, decided it must act.

NATO Takes Action

The NAC recognized the inability of the UN to settle the conflict through diplomacy

alone. The UN's previous efforts in Bosnia and now in Kosovo proved ineffective. As Leon

Malazogu, founder of Democracy for Development, argues, "The situation in Kosovo was

escalating to the point of resembling Bosnia which was an obvious indication that diplomacy was

not leading anywhere."[11] The NAC believed military force ended the conflict in Bosnia and that

Kosovo required the same response in order to stop the escalation of violence. Therefore, despite

the lack of a UN Security Council Resolution authorizing force, the NAC authorized Supreme

Allied Commander in Europe (SACEUR), Clark to begin a bombing campaign if Serbian forces

didn't withdraw from Kosovo.

On March 21, in one last diplomatic attempt, Richard Holbrooke, the United States Special Envoy to the Balkans, met personally with Milosevic. Holbrooke warned Milosevic that if he failed to comply with demands to leave Kosovo "the bombing would start."[12] Following Milosevic's refusal Holbrooke announced publically that the peace talks had failed. The Organization for Security and Cooperation in Europe (OSCE) pulled its observers out of Kosovo and a few days later Operation ALLIED FORCE, NATO's official bombing campaign, began.

Operation ALLIED FORCE

NATO estimated that the bombing would only last a few days. They anticipated a quick end to the conflict with Milosevic acting as he did in Bosnia. Unfortunately the leaders failed to understand the significance of Kosovo to Milosevic's political situation within Serbia. He could not give in and risk the perception he was weak on Serbian nationalism. To Milosevic relenting to NATO's efforts meant giving away a core piece of Serbian identity and threatened a central pillar to his hold on power. In the end Operation ALLIED FORCE lasted for 78 days during which 863,000 Kosovar Albanians were expelled from their homes and estimates of hundreds of thousands more were internally displaced.

Despite Milosevic and the Serbian forces' surrender, scholars and military leaders question whether of NATO achieved its objectives. In the United States, President William J. Clinton defined the operation's three goals as "To demonstrate the seriousness of NATO's opposition to aggression, to deter Milosevic from continuing and escalating his attacks on helpless civilians, and if need be, to damage Serbia's capacity to wage war against Kosovo by seriously diminishing its military capabilities."[13] NATO leaders demonstrated their resolve and ability to effectively respond to a crisis however their effect on Serbian military capabilities wasn't as definitive. Scholars disagree significantly on whether NATO successfully halted

Serbian violence against ethnic Albanians. A key argument for NATO intervention in Kosovo

was the need to protect ethnic Albanians from Serbian oppression yet the lack of a ground force

option for dealing with the crisis affected their ability to alter the violence against the local

population by Serb forces. It is unrealistic to assume an aerial bombing campaign alone can

effectively prevent atrocities on the ground. As Lieutenant General Michael Short (OAF Air

Component Commander) noted "we couldn't stop the killing from the air... we were not going

to be efficient or effective."[14] Dr Eliot Cohen, Director of Strategic Studies at Johns Hopkins

University, concurred with Lt Gen Short's opinion "… ALLIED FORCE represents a poor use

of air power, one which cannot and… could not achieve the central objective with which this war

began, namely the rescue of the Kosovar Albanians from mass murder, rape, and deportation."[15]

Critics of intervention argue the use of force actually did more harm than good. They

believe the removal of the Kosovo Verification Force (KVF) as an international presence

observing events on the ground in Kosovo gave Milosevic a green light to proceed with his

campaign of ethnic cleansing. A U.S. State Department report from late May 1999, revealed that

the levels of ethnic cleansing dramatically increased following the removal of observers stating

"by late March 1999 Serbian forces dramatically increased the scope and pace of their

efforts…toward a sustained and systematic effort to ethnically cleanse the entire province of

Kosovo."[16] In addition, Serbian forces were prepared to conduct a massive effort to force ethnic

Albanians from their homes prior to the start of OAF. According to General Sir Rupert Smith "in

Kosovo in 1998-99, in their direct and simplistic logic, the Yugoslavian army worked to the

same principle [as the Russians did in Chechen]: no people, no threat; hence ethnic cleansing –

which is what led to the NATO bombing over the province."[17]

Proponents of intervention argue the ethnic cleansing would've occurred anyway and that the bombing probably prevented even worse atrocities by forcing Serbian forces to deal with the airstrikes. At the 2001 Human Rights Conference of the University of Bonn, Rasmus Tenbergen noted that "Most scholars are of the opinion that further non-military options had no possibility of success... further hesitation could have led to even more human rights violations in Kosovo."[18]

It is also probable that Milosevic drove ethnic Albanians from their homes as a way to fight back against NATO forces, creating a huge exodus of refugees flooding neighboring countries in order to overwhelm NATO and force them to deal with a humanitarian aid crisis outside of Kosovo while also conducting the air campaign. Initially the bombing campaign rallied the Serbian people around Milosevic in his fight against NATO. However, as NATO expanded it's bombing to include infrastructure targets in Serbia, this support faded.

Finally, critics of OAF argue NATO's bombing didn't solve the question of Kosovo's autonomy. The ethnic conflict resulted in the commitment of NATO troops in the region for more than 10 years and there is still disagreement over Kosovo's rightful status as part of Serbia or as an independent state. . Kosovo declared its independence in 2008. Yet the international community as well as Serbs and Kosovars still disagree over Kosovo independence.[19]

The Decision to Use Force

Several factors led to NATO's decision to intervene militarily in Kosovo. Concerns over the conflict escalating and spilling over into neighboring countries posed what both NATO and the UN perceived as a threat to security and stability in the region. NATO expressed its concern over Milosevic's actions against the Kosovar people in its official *Statement on Kosovo* declaring the Former Republic of Yugoslavia's (FRY) actions were "creating a massive humanitarian catastrophe which also threatens to destabilize the surrounding region."[20] Cohen argues "The United States went to war over Kosovo-a place of almost no intrinsic value-less to curb Serb misbehavior there, than to preclude adverse consequences elsewhere, for example, a general deterioration in the relations of Balkan states that could ultimately pit Greece against Turkey, and hence, undermine NATO."[21]

For NATO this threat required military intervention and the NAC cited Article 52 of the UN Charter for justification of their actions. Article 52 states "Nothing in the present Charter precludes the existence of regional arrangements for dealing with such matters relating to the maintenance of international peace and security as are appropriate for regional action provided that such arrangements or agencies and their activities are consistent with the Purposes and Principles of the United Nations."[22] The NATO heads of State and Government statement on Kosovo claimed that their military action "supports the political aims of the international community... [and] The Foreign Minister of Germany spoke of NATO action conforming to the 'sense and logic' of such resolutions as the Security Council had managed to pass."[23] Patrick Thornberry, Professor Emeritus of International Law at Keele University, points out that "Despite the absence of a Security Council resolution explicitly authorizing or otherwise endorsing the use of force against FRY... Key phrases in NATO documents mimic the UN Charter."[24]

Despite the UN's primary purpose of maintaining international peace and security, the UN Security Council was unlikely to authorize the use of force in Kosovo. Russian support for Serbia as well as concerns that intervention violated Article 2 of the UN Charter limited the

UN's ability effectively act in the Balkans.[25] As Matthew Wyman, a specialist on Russian politics at Keele University, notes "It is clear…the United Nations Security Council is unable to act in many situations that cry out for global response, because of the idiosyncrasies of one or more of its permanent members. In Kosovo, NATO sought for the first time to step into this particular breach."[26]

In addition to concerns over threats to stability in the region, NATO's decision to act was influenced by the belief that its credibility was at stake in the crisis. NATO began in 1949 as an alliance intended to provide security for Europe against the growing threat of Soviet aggression. Following the end of the Cold War and the breakup of the Soviet Union, NATO's reason for existence came into question. The conflicts erupting among the Balkan states (Bosnia, Croatia, and now Kosovo) challenged NATO's resolve and credibility as well as its ability to provide security in the European theater. Aidan Hehir, Director of the Security and International Relations Program at the University of Westminster, noted that "the credibility of the West and NATO in particular diminished as the conflict escalated without resolution."[27]

Perhaps the most influential factor in the decision to resort to military force in Kosovo was the UN and NATO's experience in Bosnia. U.S. and NATO leaders feared that Kosovo was becoming a repeat of Bosnia and in the words of Albright "…the international community was not going to stand by and watch the Serb authorities do in Kosovo what they did in Bosnia."[28] Based on what happened in that conflict, Albright was convinced that only the threat of military force would force Milosevic to cease his violence against ethnic Albanians in Kosovo. Senator Bob Dole who supported Albright's hawkish stance, told the Senate Foreign Relations Subcommittee "In my view, the United States must lead the European powers to support a credible threat of force. Warnings, asset freezes, and other punitive economic measures are steps in the right direction-but as we saw in Bosnia, they are clearly not enough to stop Milosevic and his military police."[29] At the same meeting before the Senate Foreign Relations Committee, James Hooper, director of the Balkan Institute in Washington DC, testified "The Serbian crackdown in Kosovo presents the United States with a Bosnia-like situation. Remain in the sidelines and watch ethnic cleansing unfold, or muster the political will to intervene early and forcefully to prevent escalation, genocide, and spillover to neighboring states that will destroy NATO's credibility and upset the Dayton Peace Accords."[30] U.S. lawmakers saw the threat of military force as a viable diplomatic approach to the Kosovo crisis.

International demands that something must be done to stop human rights violations in Kosovo increased as the violence escalated. The memory of human rights atrocities in Bosnia, the recent failure by the UN to prevent genocide in Rwanda, and the U.S. experience in Somalia influenced the decision to take action in Kosovo. President Clinton supported the view that human rights violations required swift, firm action. In his argument to the NY Times, he stated "make no mistake, if we and our allies do not have the will to act, there will be more massacres. In dealing with aggressors in the Balkans, hesitation is a license to kill. But action and resolve save lives."[31]

Blair agreed the international community must intervene to stop the ethnic cleansing in Kosovo. In his view 2,000 deaths in Kosovo in the 12 months prior to OAF was equal to genocide and "genocide can never be a purely internal matter."[32] Blair further argued that the resulting "massive flows of refugees which unsettle neighboring countries" is a threat to international peace and security and is therefore further justification to intervene.[33]

Michael Walzer in "Just and Unjust Wars" argues that "Humanitarian intervention is justified when it is a response (with reasonable expectations of success) to acts "that shock the moral conscience of mankind."[34] Robert Di Prizio believes that in the case of Operation ALLIED FORCE "No explicit, widely accepted controlling legal authority, such as a UNSC resolution authorized intervention, but a strong case can be made that a combination of recent precedents of "humanitarian intervention, a growing international concern for human rights and humanitarian, and traditional just war rationale justified and intervention…."[35] In the UK, the comparison to intervention in Northern Iraq in 1991 was used to support intervention in Kosovo. A UK Foreign Office in November 1998 cited the precedent for "legitimacy of a limited use of force in support of purposes laid down by the Security Council but without the Council's express authorization in order to avert a humanitarian catastrophe."[36] Thus NATO justified intervention on the grounds that Kosovo presented both a moral imperative to act based on humanitarian reasons and threatened the security and stability of the area.

Changing International Views on Sovereignty and Government Responsibility

Despite the lack of a UNSC resolution authorizing the use of force in Kosovo there was a growing consensus in the international community that governments have a responsibility to protect their citizens. Reflecting on OAF and NATO's military intervention, Ted Carpenter, Senior Fellow for Defense and Foreign Policy Studies at the Cato Institute states "When a government violates the rights of its citizens the way the Milosevic regime violated the rights of the Albanians, the international community has a right and even an obligation to intervene with military force."[37] Interestingly in the UN "all except one member of the Security Council (China) accepted that the Yugoslav government had a responsibility to protect its Kosovar Albanian citizens from grave breaches of international humanitarian law…and that… it fell to the Security Council to adopt measures aimed at ending the violence and settling the dispute in a manner that protected the legitimate rights and interests of Kosovo's ethnic groups."[38] In a 1999 article for the Economist former UN Secretary General Kofi Annan acknowledged this international obligation when he stated "States are now widely understood to be instruments at the service of their peoples, and not vice versa…When we read the Charter today, we are more than ever conscious that its aim is to protect individual human beings, not to protect those who abuse them."[39]

The growing belief in the obligation of the international community to involve itself with domestic conflicts within other nations reflects a new understanding of sovereignty. The traditional approach towards sovereignty is based on the Treaty of Westphalia. The Treaty (comprised of the Peace of Westphalia and the Peace of Osnabruck) marked the end of Europe's 30 Years War and established the concept of the sovereign state based upon geography and political affinity, not nationality. [40] This principle dominated international law since its inception in 1648. Alynna Lyon, Associate Professor of Political Science at the University of New Hampshire, points out that this understanding of sovereignty prohibits interference in the domestic affairs of another country without a clear invitation to do so.[41] Article 2(7) of the UN Charter also supports this traditional view.

In contrast to this traditional view, Blair, argued "global interconnectedness created a global responsibility to deal with egregious human suffering. Sovereigns acquired responsibilities to international society because domestic problems caused by massive human rights abuse, for example, spread across borders."[42] Brown University's Amir Pasic and Thomas Weiss further contend "When the fabric of a community's consent for aid is problematic; its weakened condition does not allow it to respond as it might in less trying times."[43] Therefore an invitation may not be possible in the midst of a crisis.

A.J Bellamy, the Senior Lecturer in peace and Conflict Studies at the University of Queensland, supports the concept of sovereignty that includes government responsibility to protect the rights of its citizens and he justifies international intervention when governments fail in this responsibility. He writes "Only those states that cherish, nurture, and protect the fundamental rights of their citizens and thereby fulfill their sovereign responsibility are entitled to the full panoply of sovereign rights. By this view sovereignty is not suspended or overridden when international society acts against (or to assist) a government that fails in its responsibilities by abusing its citizens on a massive scale."[44] Bellamy's concept of sovereignty as responsibility is based on two main ideas; first that human rights are inherent to being a human and these are universal and equal for all people. Secondly, when these rights are abused, the international community has a responsibility to protect people from such abuse.[45]

NATO's actions in Operation ALLIED FORCE raised the issue of intervention in sovereign states in order to protect human rights. The question evolved beyond whether or not states have a responsibility to protect the rights of their citizens or even if the international community should somehow intervene when states abuse their own citizens. Rather the issue became timely intervention and what form such intervention should take. Indeed as Blair remarked "The most pressing foreign policy problem we face is to identify the circumstances in which we should get actively involved in other people's conflicts."[46]

In an attempt to address this issue the Canadian government established the International Commission on Intervention and State sovereignty (ICISS) in 2000. The committee presented its report titled "The Responsibility to Protect" (R2P) to the UN in December 2001. This doctrine upholds the responsibility of a sovereign government to protect its citizens and the responsibility of the international community to intervene when a government fails to do so. R2P continues to require UN authorization for intervention. It also states that prior to using military force, the international community has a responsibility to prevent situations where intervention becomes necessary. It further outlines measures to take short of military action and emphasizes the responsibility to rebuild after intervention by military force.[47]

U.S. Traditional Approach to Use of Military Force

The United States traditionally views the decision to go to war as based upon vital national interests. This idea was codified in the first principle of former U.S. Secretary of Defense Casper Weinberger's Doctrine on the use of force and is reinforced in the Powell Doctrine. However this "American Way of War" is difficult to apply in humanitarian interventions such as Kosovo. James Kurth, a senior fellow at the Foreign Policy Research Institute (Philadelphia) sees "Humanitarian intervention as a rejection of the Weinberger-Powell doctrine governing the use of force."[48] Eliot Cohen argues the war in Kosovo is evidence that America's traditional approach to war is "inadequate and indeed obsolete" and furthermore "Kosovo demonstrates the extent to which the circumstances of a post Cold-War era have obliged American military and civilian leaders to extemporize an approach to war that differs radically from past practice…."[49] If Kurth and Cohen are correct then the United States needs specific doctrine to guide U.S. military and civilian leaders confronted with decisions on intervention in humanitarian crises.

Prior to the war in Kosovo, President Clinton established broad guidelines to address humanitarian intervention decisions. He outlined these guidelines in his May 1994 Presidential Decision Directive/NSC-25. This now unclassified guidance provides insight into U.S. support for UN Peace Operations Resolutions. The U.S. involvement in Somalia influenced this guidance which President Clinton developed during the 1994 genocide in Rwanda. In PDD-25 President Clinton identified "humanitarian disasters requiring urgent action, coupled with violence" as well as "sudden and unexpected interruption of established democracy or gross violation of human rights, coupled with violence or the threat thereof" as factors to consider when determining support for UN Peace Operations Resolutions. He also states that the political, economic, and humanitarian consequences of inaction must be considered.[50] Considering the guidance in this PDD and the public explanations for intervention in Kosovo, the U.S. employed a newly developed approach to U.S. intervention based not only on traditional national security threat reasons but also upon human rights considerations.

This policy shift reflects the tension within U.S. foreign policy. This tension is between a desire to remain free of external foreign commitments that require the nation's involvement in non-existential threats (isolationism) and the perception that America is the guardian and promoter of human rights (based on our Declaration of Independence that proclaims these rights are universal). From George Washington's presidency to Operation DESERT STORM, U.S. foreign policy shifted between these two approaches. However, U.S. involvement remained largely based upon threats to our national security and interests. The war in Kosovo marked a shift towards intervention based more on humanitarian concerns rather than clear existential threats to the nation. President Barak H. Obama reflected this shift in approach in his Nobel Prize speech stating "force can be justified on humanitarian grounds...[because] inaction tears at our conscience and can lead to more costly intervention later."[51] This concern for human rights influenced the U.S. decision to support UN resolution 1973 in 2011. This resolution referred to R2P doctrine as a basis for establishing a no-fly zone over Libya and "authorizing all necessary measures" to defend Libyan civilians. Obama clearly supported the R2P doctrine's applicability to the Libyan crisis in his 21 March 2011 statement, "The core principle that has to be upheld is when there is a potential humanitarian crisis about to take place … we can't simply stand by with empty words; that we have to take some sort of action."[52] This is the same justification used in 1999 by President Clinton in response to the crisis in Kosovo.

Yet the United States has not codified its responses to humanitarian crises. The U.S. remained uninvolved militarily in Tunisia and Egypt's Arab Spring uprisings, preferring to rely more heavily upon traditional diplomatic means of intervention. These movements reflected more of a desire for self-determination among citizens rather than clear humanitarian rights violations and the U.S. response followed the more traditional distant, non-interventionist approach to foreign policy. However, the current situation in Syria presents both a situation of human rights violations and a movement for self-determination. Unfortunately the lack of clear doctrine for U.S. decision makers hampers U.S. policy and creates a no-win situation for the current U.S. administration. Thus far President Obama hasn't resorted to R2P doctrine to sway his approach. It will be interesting to observe international and U.S. ongoing responses to the crisis.

Future Humanitarian Intervention

In the future the U.S. will continue to face decisions of whether to intervene or not in a variety of crises around the world. The first step in the decision making process is the determination whether intervention is justified or not. A simple decision matrix may be applied here. If a situation arises where intervention is prohibited under international law and there is no moral or ethical obligation to intervene then the US should not intervene. An example of such a situation is internal conflict within a sovereign nation in which neither vital U.S. interests exist nor national security is threatened, as well as that there is no evidence of human rights violations.

In contrast crises may occur where international law allows intervention and a moral imperative exists (such as in cases of genocide or ethnic cleansing by an illegitimate government). In these cases intervention is not only allowed it may also be required of developed nations. Leon Malazogu states it well, "Solving conflict through non-violent means is the most desirable method. However, there are circumstances under which one is ethically bound to use force as a last resort to stop a greater evil."[53]

The most difficult situations arise when the legality of intervention is not clear yet a moral imperative to intervene exists. These situations require careful consideration of the cost of intervention as well as the cost of inaction. Any decision to act must account for both international law and moral obligation. International support for intervention, the ability to improve the situation through intervention, and the likelihood of success must determine how and what type of intervention is most appropriate.

In order for the use of force to be just in any conflict, the U.S. must exhaust all other avenues of intervention prior to military force. The cost in human lives both to our own forces as well as to civilians on the ground must never be taken lightly. As Matthew Wyman notes, "To justify a military response to this humanitarian outrage, one clearly needs to be satisfied that all other avenues had been closed off."[54]

In addition the likelihood of success must be considered when deciding to intervene. In the case of Operation ALIED FORCE critics argue that NATO's actions made the situation worse and that an aerial bombing campaign alone wasn't able to stop the atrocities. Prior to intervening in future crises the U.S. must examine whether the military force used is appropriate given the situation and determine its likelihood to succeed. According to Jane Stromseth, "In order to have a reasonable prospect of success in stopping atrocities…[there] must be clear-eyed analysis of the underlying conflict and a plausible military concept of operations…"[55] Ideally sound doctrine and a thorough historical understanding of a conflict will inform this analysis of the success probability and the best means of force. In the case of OAF the enduring rivalry between ethnic Albanians and Serbians in Kosovo continued with human rights violations committed upon Serbians as they fled the territory. As A.J. Lyon points out, "…Kosovo illustrated how ending the violence does not always end the suffering…"[56] NATO needed a better understanding of the history of conflict prior to and following the bombing campaign in order to effectively prevent continuing human rights violations.

Finally, intervention requires international support, especially by the UN or allies in the affected region. The U.S. must seek the support of other nations when determining the necessity of humanitarian intervention. International support is critical to successful intervention operations and especially to post conflict resolution and the restoration of a stable and secure state that ensures justice and human rights are preserved.

Conclusions

While each conflict involving humanitarian intervention is unique and no single approach to humanitarian intervention is possible, a military doctrine to guide decision makers on the use of force in humanitarian crises can be developed. Doctrine is descriptive, not prescriptive and therefore it is not a checklist to be followed in every situation. It requires judgment and must be based on prior experiences. The United States has a wealth of experience, both positive and negative, to draw upon in developing such a doctrine.

The cost of intervening in conflicts in foreign nations is high. Political considerations, both at home and abroad must be included in decision-making but nations must also consider their moral obligations to intervene. As a world power, the United States' actions will set a precedent for intervention by other nations. Our justification must be based on sound decision making with an emphasis on concern for protecting human rights and promoting justice. The use of military force may be a valid response but other approaches must be exhausted before undertaking military operations. In addition, international support and involvement needs to be a part of the intervention and follow up plan.

Unfortunately, humanitarian crises continue to challenge the international community. The recent Arab Spring uprisings, conflict in northern Africa, and the civil war in Syria are recent examples of crises. The United States cannot predict every future crisis nor can it respond the same way to each one. However, the development of a thorough, well developed doctrine based on previous experience, considering both traditional and current concepts of sovereignty, and the responsibility of the international community to protect human rights must be pursued. The potential cost in blood and treasure of failing to do otherwise are too high.

Notes

[1] Zidas Daskolovski, "*Claims to Kosovo: Nationalism and Self-Determination*" in Florain Bieber and Zidas Daskolovski, eds., *Understanding the War in Kosovo* (London: Frank Cass Publishers, 2003), 14-15.

[2] Alexsander Pavkovic, "Kosovo/Kosova: A Land of conflicting Myths" in Michael Waller, Kyril Drezov and Bulent Gokay, eds., .*Politics of Disillusion* (London: Frank Cass Publishers, 2001), 7.

[3] Daskalovski, 19.

[4] ibid, 20.

[5] ibid, 17.

[6] US Dept of State Fact Sheet, 95/11/01.

[7] Wesley Clark, *Waging Modern War* (United States: PublicAffairs, 2001), 153.

[8] Stefan Wolff, "The Limits of Non-Military International Intervention: A Case Study of the Kosovo Conflict" in Florain Bieber and Zidas Daskolovski, eds., *Understanding the War in Kosovo* (London: Frank Cass Publishers, 2003), 89

[9] Aidan Hehir, ed. In his introduction to *Kosovo, Intervention and State building* (New York: Routledge, 2010), 7.

[10] Michael Waller, Kyril Drezov and Bulent Gokay, ed., *.Politics of Disillusion* (London: Frank Cass Publishers, 2001), 104.

[11] Leon Malazogu, "When Doves Support War and Hawks Oppose It: An Analysis of Humanitarian Intervention in Kosova" in Florain Bieber and Zidas Daskolovski, eds., *Understanding the War in Kosovo* (London: Frank Cass Publishers, 2003), 133.

[12] Hosmer, 20.

[13] Benjamin S. Lambeth, *NATO's Air War for Kosovo: A Strategic and Operational Assessment* (Santa Monica, CA: Rand, 2001), 19.

[14] Bruce R. Pirnie, Alan Vick, Adam Grissom, Karl P. Mueller, and David T. Orletsky. *Beyond Close Air Support: Forging a New Air-Ground Partnership (*Santa Monica, CA: Rand, 2005), 40.

[15] *"United States and NATO Military Operations Against the Federal Republic of Yugoslavia.": Hearing before the House Armed Services Subcommittee*, 106th Congress, 10 (1999) (Dr Eliot Cohen, Director of Strategic Studies, Johns Hopkins University).

[16] Carpenter, 53.

[17] Sir Rupert Smith, *The Utility of Force: The Art of War in the Modern World* (New York: Random House/Vintage Books, 2008), 281.

[18] RasmusTenbergen, "Bombs for Human Rights? Humanitarian Intervention in Kosovo."(lecture, Human Rights Conference of the University of Bonn and the Institute for Leadership Development, June 2001), 11.

[19] Ted Galen Carpenter, ed., NATO's *Empty Victory* (Washington D.C.: Cato Institute, 2000), 55.

[20] Patrick Thornberry, "Come Friendly bombs… : International Law in Kosovo" in Michael Waller, Kyril Drezov and Bulent Gokay, ed., *.Politics of Disillusion* (London, Frank Cass Publishers, 2001), 50.

[21] Eliot Cohen, *"Kosovo the New American Way of War"* in Andrew J. Bacevich and Eliot A Cohen, eds, *War Over Kosovo* (New York: Columbia University Press, 2001), 46.

[22] "Charter of the United Nations and Statute of the International Court of Justice," (Mount Vernon, NY: Peter Pauper Press, 1945), Chapter VII, Article 52.

[23] Thornberry, 46.

[24] Thornberry, 45.

[25] Article 2(4) of the Charter states that "all members of the UN shall refrain in their international relations from the threat or use of force against the territorial integrity or political independence of any state, or in any manner inconsistent with the Purposes of the United Nations."

[26] Matthew Wyman, "Kosovo: Why Intervention was Right" in Michael Waller, Kyril Drezov and Bulent Gokay,

eds., .*Politics of Disillusion* (London: Frank Cass Publishers, 2001), 108.

[27] Hehir, 7.

[28] Robert C. Di Prizio, *Armed Humanitarians: US Interventions from Northern Iraq to Kosovo.* (Baltimore: John Hopkins University Press, 2002), 136.

[29] Senator Bob Dole, prepared statement to the Senate Foreign Relations subcommittee on European Affairs, 6 May 1998.

[30] James R. Hooper, U.S. Congress. Senate. "The Crisis in Kosovo." Hearings before the Senate Foreign Relations Subcommittee on European Affairs, 105th Congress, 6 May and 24 June, 1998, 19-20.

[31] Carpenter, 51.

[32] Carpenter, 177.

[33] Carpenter, 178.

[34] Michael Walzer, *Just and Unjust War.* (New York: Basic Books, 1977), 107.

[35] Di Prizio, 136.

[36] Thornberry 46.

[37] Carpenter, 107.

[38] Alex J. Bellamy, "Kosovo and the advent of sovereignty as responsibility" in Aidan Hehir, ed. *Kosovo, Intervention and State building* (New York: Routledge, 2010), 51.

[39] Kofi Annan, "Two Concepts of Sovereignty" in *The Economist*, 18 September 1999, 49.

[40] Treaty of Westphalia, (Peace Treaty Between the Holy Roman Emperor and the King of France and the Respectve Allies) 1648. The Avalon Project: Documents in History, Law, and Diplomacy. Lillian Goldman Law Library, Yale University. Accessed 2 April 2013. http://avalon.law.yale.edu/17th_century/westphal.asp

[41] Alynna J. Lyon and Mary Fran T. Malone, "Responding to Kosovo's call for humanitarian intervention" in Aidan Hehir, ed. *Kosovo, Intervention and State building* (New York: Routledge, 2010), 17.

[42] Bellamy, 43.

[43] Amir Pasic and Thomas G. Weiss, "The Politics of Rescue: Yugoslavia's Wars and the Humanitarian Impulse" in Anthony F. Long Jr, ed., *Just Intervention*(Washington, DC: Georgetown University Press, 2003), 118.

[44] Bellamy, 40.

[45] Bellamy, 40

[46] Carpenter, 177.

[47] Report of the International Commission on Intervention and State Sovereignty, *The Responsibility to Protect*, (Ottawa, Canada: 2001)

[48] James Kurth, *"First War of the Global Era"* in Andrew J. Bacevich and Eliot A. Cohen, eds. *War Over Kosovo* (New York: Columbia University Press, 2001), 82.

[49] Cohen, 45.

[50] U.S. President. Presidential Decision Directive/ NSC-25, Annex I, B

[51] Massimo Calabresi, "Susan Rice: A Voice for Intervention," *Time* 24 Mar 2011, http://www.time.com/magazine

[52] Calabresi

[53] Malazogu, 127

[54] Wyman, 104.

[55] Jane Stromseth, "Rethinking Humanitarian Intervention" in J.L. Holzgrefe and Robert O. Keohane, eds. *Humanitarian Intervention: Ethical, Legal and Political Dilemmas* (Cambridge: Cambridge Universtiy Press, 2003), 269.

[56] Lyon, 34.

Bibliography

Annan, Kofi. (1999, Sep 18). "International: Two concepts of sovereignty." *The Economist,* 352, 49-50.

Bacevich, Andrew J. and Eliot A. Cohen eds. *War over Kosovo.* New York: Columbia University Press, 2001.

Bellamy, Alex J. *Kosovo and International Society.* New York: Palgrave Macmillan, 2002.

Bieber, Florian, and Zidas Daskalovski eds. *Understanding the War in Kosovo.* London: Frank Cass Publishers, 2003.

Calabresi, Massimo, "Susan Rice: A Voice for Intervention." *Time,* 24 March 2011, http:///www.time.com

Carpenter, Ted Galen ed. *NATO's Empty Victory.* Washington DC: Cato Institute, 2000.

Chandler, David. *From Kosovo to Kabul: Human Rights and International Intervention.* Sterling, VA: Pluto Press, 2002

Charter of the United Nations and Statute of the International Court of Justice. Mount Vernon, NY: Peter Pauper Press, 1945.

Chomsky, Noam. *The New Military Humanism: Lessons from Kosovo.* Monroe, ME: Common Courage Press, 1999

Clark, Wesley Gen. *Waging Modern War.* United States: PublicAffairs, 2001.

Cordesman, Anthony H. *The Lessons and Non-Lessons of the Air and Missile Campaign in Kosovo.* Westport, CT: Praeger, 2001.

Di Prizio, Robert C. *Armed Humanitarians: US Interventions from Northern Iraq to Kosovo.* Baltimore: John Hopkins University Press, 2002.

Daalder, Ivo H. and Michael E. O'Hanlon. *Winning Ugly: NATO's War to Save Kosovo.* Washington, DC: Brookings institute Press, 2000

Duizings, Ger. *Religion and the Politics of Identity in Kosovo.* New York: Columbia University Press, 2000.

Hehir, Aidan. *Humanitarian Intervention After Kosovo: Iraq, Darfur and the Record of Global Civil Society.* New York: Palgrave Macmillan, 2008.

Hehir, Aidan. *Intervention and Statebuilding: the international community and the transition to independence.* New York: Palgrave Macmillan, 2010.

Hehir, Aidan . *The Responsibility to Protect: Rhetoric, Reality and the Future of Humanitarian Intervention.* New York: Palgrave Macmillan, 2012.

Henriksen, Dag. *NATO's Gamble.* Annapolis, MD: Naval Institute Press, 2007.

Holzgrefe, J.L. and Robert O. Keohane. eds. *Humanitarian Intervention: Ethical, Legal and Political Dilemmas.* New York: Cambridge University Press, 2003

Hosmer, Stephen T. *The Conflict over Kosovo: why Milosevic decided to settle when he did.* Santa Monica, CA: Rand, 2001.

Houghton, David Patrick. *The Decision Point: Six cases in U.S. foreign policy decision-making.* New York: Oxford University Press, 2013

Lamb, Michael W. Sr., Lt Col. "Operation Allied Force: Golden Nuggets for Future Campaigns." Air War College, Maxwell Paper No. 27, 2002.

Lambeth, Benjamin S. *NATO's Air War for Kosovo: A Strategic and Operational Assessment.* Santa Monica, CA: Rand, 2001.

Lang Jr., Anthony F. ed. *Just Intervention.* Washington, DC: Georgetown University Press, 2003.

Morton, Jeffrey S., R. Craig Nation, Paul Forage, and Stefano Bianchini eds. *Reflections on the Balkan Wars: Ten Years After the Break Up of Yugoslavia.* New York: Palgrave Macmillan, 2004

Nardulli, Bruce R., Walter L. Perry, Bruce Pirnie, John Gordon IV, and John G. McGinn. *Disjointed War: Military Operations in Kosovo, 1999.* Santa Monica, CA: Rand, 2002.

Nelan, Bruce. "Into the Fire", *Time,* 5 April 1999 http://www.time.com/

Perritt Jr., Henry H. *Kosovo Liberation Army: the inside story of an insurgency.* Urbana, Illinois: University of Illinois Press, 2008

Peters, John E., Stuart Johnson, Nora Bensahel, Timothy Liston, and Traci Williams. *European Contributions to Operation Allied Force.* Santa Monica, CA: Rand, 2001.

Pirnie, Bruce R., Alan Vick, Adam Grissom, Karl P. Mueller, and David T. Orletsky. *Beyond Close Air Support: Forging a New Air-Ground Partnership.* Santa Monica, CA: Rand, 2005.

Report of the International Commission on Intervention and State Sovereignty, *The Responsibility to Protect*, Ottawa, Canada: 2001.

Saariluoman, Katarina. *Operation Allied Force: A Case of Humanitarian Intervention?* Garmisch-Partenkirchen, Germany: Partnership for Peace Consortium of Defense Academies and Security Studies Institutes, Athena Papers, September 2004.

Schnabel, Albrecht and Ramesh Thakur eds. *Kosovo and the Challenge of Humanitarian Intervention.* New York: United Nations University Press, 2000

Smith, Rupert Gen. *The Utility of Force*: *The Art of War in the Modern World.* New York: Random House/Vintage Books, 2008.

Tenbergen, Rasmus. "Bombs for Human Rights? Humanitarian Intervention in Kosovo." Paper presented at the Human Rights Conference of the University of Bonn and the Institute for Leadership Development, June 2001.

Treaty of Westphalia, (Peace Treaty Between the Holy Roman Emperor and the King of France and the Respectve Allies) 1648. The Avalon Project: Documents in History, Law, and Diplomacy. Lillian Goldman Law Library, Yale University. Accessed 2 April 2013. http://avalon.law.yale.edu/17th_century/westphal.asp

United States Air Force, Headquarters. "The Air War over Serbia: Aero space Power in Operation Allied Force." Initial Report

U.S. Congress. House. *United States and NATO Military Operations Against the Federal Republic of Yugoslavia.: Hearing before the House Armed Services Subcommittee*, 106th Congress, 1999.

U.S. Congress. Senate. *The Crisis in Kosovo.: Hearings before the Senate Foreign Relations Subcommittee on European Affairs,* 105th Congress, 6 May and 24 June, 1998.

U.S. Congress. Senate. "The War in Kosovo and a Postwar Analysis." Hearings before the Senate Foreign Relations Committee, 106th Congress, 20 April, 28 September, and 6 October, 1999.

U.S. President. "Decision Directive/NSC-25," (3 May 1994).

Waller, Michael, Kyril Drezov, and Bulent Gokay, ed. *Kosovo: The Politics of Delusion.* London: Frank Cass Publishers, 2001.